T0287156

PAST & PRESENT

CARSON CITY

Opposite: This c. 1920s view of Carson City from Carson Hill shows a growing capital city. At the time, the area surrounding Carson City was largely used for agricultural purposes. The Lompa Ranch can be seen to the back left. Until recently, the ranch was one of the last remaining cattle ranches in the Carson City area. (Courtesy of the Nevada Department of Transportation.)

PAST & PRESENT

CARSON CITY

Alexis K. Thomas

Copyright © 2023 by Alexis K. Thomas
ISBN 978-1-4671-6009-4

Library of Congress Control Number: 2023937797

Published by Arcadia Publishing
Charleston, South Carolina

Printed in the United States of America

For all general information, please contact Arcadia Publishing:
Telephone 843-853-2070
Fax 843-853-0044
E-mail sales@arcadiapublishing.com

Visit us on the Internet at www.arcadiapublishing.com

ON THE FRONT COVER: The Briggs House, now known as the Fox Brewery, has had many names over its lifetime. Originally constructed in 1862 in the Italianate style, the building was occupied by the St. Charles Hotel and Muller's Hotel. In 1895, the two hotels were merged by Gilbert and Dorcas Briggs to create the Briggs House. During the early 20th century, all ornamentation was removed from the building, then known as the New Hotel Page, a hotel, casino, and cocktail lounge. Today, it looks much like it did in the 1890s. (Both, author's collection.)

ON THE BACK COVER: Two automobiles sit along the Reno-Carson Highway around the 1920s. (Courtesy of the Nevada Department of Transportation.)

Contents

ACKNOWLEDGMENTS

This book illustrating Carson City's evolution as a city would not exist without the assistance of the Nevada Department of Transportation, which allowed me access to and the use of their extensive historic photograph collection. Each photograph provided is credited at the end of the caption. All present images were photographed by the author.

Thank you to Michael Harms for exploring Carson City with me, researching photograph locations, and critiquing present images so each one allows for a precise historic comparison. Additional thanks to Arcadia Publishing for providing me the opportunity to publish my first book and to Caroline (Anderson) Vickerson for trying her hardest to keep me on schedule.

INTRODUCTION

In September 1858, Abraham Curry and three partners purchased most of what would become Carson City for $500 and some horses. They soon laid out a townsite, naming it after Kit Carson. Discovery of the Comstock Lode in 1859 provided additional incentive for the development of the town. The first post office opened on November 18, 1858, and Carson City quickly became the hub of a network of toll roads and freight and stage lines. It was a station for the short-lived Pony Express of 1860–1861, a station on the subsequent Overland Telegraph line, and a stop on the 1860s Overland Stage Route.

In March 1861, the Territory of Nevada was created, and Carson City immediately became the center of its political affairs. On November 25, 1861, Carson City became the county seat of the newly created Ormsby County. In September 1863, the residents of the Nevada Territory voted to become a state and in March 1864, the US Congress approved an act enabling the residents of the Nevada Territory to form a constitution. Approved by voters in September 1864, the new Nevada State Constitution established Carson City as the state capital of Nevada. On October 31, 1864, with admission of Nevada as a state, Carson City's role as a state capital became official.

During the 1860s, Carson City was an important center for the lumber industry, as a thriving logging industry had rooted itself in the Carson Range and Lake Tahoe Basin. Ranching and farming became increasingly important in the Washoe, Eagle, and Carson Valleys with the increase of emigrant traffic through Nevada to California, as well as the increase in population due to the thriving mining and lumber industries. The Virginia & Truckee Railroad was constructed between Virginia City and Carson City from 1870 to 1871, and a number of mills for reducing and smelting Comstock ore were established along the Carson River from Empire City, east to Dayton.

During the 1880s, the decline of the Comstock Lode led to a decline of surrounding communities, including Carson City. By 1900, lumbering in the Carson Range and Lake Tahoe Basin had ended. Despite the introduction of modern systems, such as telephones and electricity to the area, Carson City's population dropped from about 4,000 to just over 2,000 people between 1890 and 1900. After 1900, transportation became an important aspect of Carson City's economy. In 1906, the Virginia & Truckee Railroad established a branch line south to Minden and up to Reno. In 1913, the establishment of the Lincoln Highway and the growing enthusiasm for automobile travel brought tourism to the city, creating another important industry for the area. Carson City's position near Lake Tahoe, a destination for locals and tourists alike, would only increase the city's appeal to travelers.

Despite an increase in travel and tourism through Carson City, it remained a small town until well after World War II, when the population reached nearly 2,000 in 1960. Since the 1960s, Carson City has continued to grow, expanding east towards Dayton and south toward Minden and Gardnerville.

CHAPTER 1

GOVERNMENT

Highway department personnel gather on the steps of the capitol building in Carson City around 1920. During the highway department's earliest days, department staff was located in the capitol building, the state printing office, and the old armory. (Past image, courtesy of Nevada Department of Transportation.)

The US Mint was Nevada's largest building at the time of its construction in 1866. It was built using sandstone from a nearby quarry. Decorative elements are from both the Classical and Italianate schools of architecture. The building was converted into the Nevada State Museum in 1959, and a two-story wing was added. (Past image, courtesy of Nevada Department of Transportation.)

The Nevada State Capitol, designed by Joseph Gosling, was constructed in 1871 in the Neoclassical Italianate style with a cruciform plan. It was constructed using sandstone, and an octagonal dome topped with a cupola surmounted the building. During 1906, an octagonal addition was added to the rear (east) of the capitol to house the state library. Additions to the northern and southern side, designed by Frederic DeLongchamps, were completed by 1915. It housed the Nevada Legislature until 1971, when the new legislature building was constructed. Presently, it continues to house the governor's office. (Past image, author's collection.)

This c. 1920s photograph shows the State Capitol building from King Street, between Carson and Curry streets. The capitol's cupola can be seen in the background. This block of King Street would become the grounds for Nevada's Supreme Court and Library in the 1930s, creating a complex of official buildings that includes the Ormsby County Courthouse and the Heroes Memorial Building. (Past image, courtesy of Nevada Department of Transportation.)

The Nevada State Orphan's Home was located on the south side of Fifth Street, between Stewart Street and Roop Street, on the site of the original children's home. Construction of the home began in 1903 and was completed in early 1905. The Classical-style building, designed by W.H. Kirk of the Virginia & Truckee Railroad, was constructed using stone and consisted of two stories with a cupola and flagpole at the center. The name was changed to the Nevada State Children's Home in 1951. The home was demolished in 1963 and replaced with cottages to remove the institutional feel. (Past image, courtesy of Nevada Department of Transportation.)

The US Post Office located along Carson Street was designed by Mifflin E. Bell and constructed from 1888 to 1891 in the Romanesque Revival style. When it was completed, it housed the US District Court, the land office, the US Weather Bureau, and the post office. In 1999, it was renamed the Paul Laxalt State Building for former Nevada governor Paul Laxalt and now houses the Nevada Commission on Tourism. (Past image, author's collection)

GOVERNMENT

The Nevada Governor's Mansion was constructed in 1909 in the Classical Revival style. It was designed by George A. Ferris, a Reno-based architect, and constructed by Friedhoff, Hoeffel, and Company. The second story possesses a balcony that extends along the east and south sides and is supported by Ionic capitals. It was remodeled in 1967 to include heating and air-conditioning. (Past image, courtesy of the Nevada Department of Transportation.)

The Nevada State Printing Office was constructed between 1885 and 1886, just east of the capitol building. It was designed by Reno architect Morill J. Curtis. It is the second-oldest state-built structure in the capitol complex and was constructed using sandstone from the Nevada State Prison quarry. It served as the state printing office until 1964. It is now part of the Nevada State Library and Archives. The building was listed in the National Register of Historic Places in 1978. (Past image, author's collection.)

Facing north on Carson Street near the intersection of Second Street, this block would become a complex of official buildings. The highway department building can be seen in the left foreground, and the county courthouse can be seen in the center background. Both were constructed in the 1920s in the Classical Revival style. The Supreme Court and Library building was constructed between the two in 1936, eliminating King Street. Today, this block remains very much the same. (Past image, author's collection.)

The Heroes Memorial Building was constructed in the Classical Revival style between 1920 and 1922. The building housed offices for the state's highway department and the attorney general's office, among other departments. In 1936, a larger materials testing laboratory for the highway department was constructed on the western (rear) side of the building in the Moderne style. (Past image, courtesy of the Nevada Department of Transportation.)

The Ormsby County Court House was constructed between 1920 and 1922 in the Classical Revival style and mirrors that of the Heroes Memorial Building to the south along the same block. Both buildings were designed by Frederick DeLongchamps while he served as the Nevada state architect. Like other government structures built around the same time, it was constructed using locally source sandstone. Today, the building still operates as the courthouse. (Past image, courtesy author's collection.)

SUPREME COURT AND LIBRARY CARSON CITY NEV.

The Supreme Court and Library, located at 100 North Carson Street, was constructed in 1936 in the Art Deco style and features the Greek key motif around the cornice as well as the Zig Zag motif. It was designed by Frederick DeLongchamps. The building has undergone very little renovations since it was originally constructed. It was listed in the National Register of Historic Places, along with the Heroes Memorial Building and the Ormsby County Courthouse House. (Past image, courtesy author's collection.)

The Nevada Legislative Building was originally constructed in 1970 along Carson Street. It was built in response to the growing legislative body, and rather than adding onto the capitol building itself, it was decided to construct a separate structure. Graham Erskine of the firm Ferris & Erskine was hired to design the building. The original design was a Mid-Century design with geometric details, such as alternating vertical panels of aggregate and white stucco with projecting white concrete panels over the windows. The building was altered again in 1995, completely renovating the exterior of the structure. (Past image, courtesy author's collection.)

Nevada Legislative Building

The capitol building's annex, located at the rear of the capitol building, was constructed in 1904. The annex contains many of the same design elements as the capitol and was constructed in an octagonal shape. In 1970, a new three-story building was constructed to east of the annex using a more contemporary design. (Past image, courtesy of the Nevada Department of Transportation.)

CHAPTER 2

RAILROADS

This c. 1940s photograph shows a Virginia & Truckee Railroad engine in Washoe Valley, north of Carson City. Construction of the railroad began in Virginia City in 1868, reaching Reno by 1872. The railroad was largely used as freight transportation to and from the Comstock Lode; however, the segment through Washoe Valley was popular for its passenger service. Service along this segment was discontinued in 1950, and the rails were removed by 1973. (Past image, courtesy of the Nevada Department of Transportation.)

The railroad established its yard and depot near the corner of Washington Street and Plaza Street in the 1870s. The yard had 40 buildings, including an icehouse, derrick house, paint house, freight house, and roundhouse. The freight house was located along Caroline Street, south of the yard. (Past image, courtesy of the Nevada Department of Transportation.)

The maintenance shop building was constructed by Abraham Curry of locally sourced sandstone in a U shape, with corrugated iron roofing. The east end contained the enginehouse; a carpentry shop and foundry were located in the north wing; and a maintenance shop, blacksmith, pattern shop, storage room, boiler room, generator, and a small office were located in the south wing. The turntable is present in the right foreground. (Past image, courtesy of the Nevada Department of Transportation.)

With the decline of the railroad line between Carson City and Virginia City during the 1920s and 1930s, the roundhouse fell into disrepair and was ultimately demolished in the late 1980s. The land was never developed and has sat vacant for almost 40 years. (Past image, courtesy of the Nevada Department of Transportation.)

The Carson City Depot for the Virginia & Truckee Railroad was located at the corner of Carson and Washington Streets. It was constructed in 1872 using a standard railroad depot plan. Over time, small alterations were made to the building, including a small shed on the rear elevation. In 1952, the Carson City Freemasons Masonic Lodge purchased the building, and it has since been used as both a meeting hall and commercial space. (Past image, courtesy of Nevada Department of Transportation.)

From Carson City to Reno, the railroad ran through Washoe Valley and the towns of Mills Station and Franktown. Mills Station was established in the early 1860s as one of the earliest logging and fluming centers in the valley. The railroad constructed a siding and freight depot in Mills Station to operate as a lumber stop. By 1881, many of the residents had left the area as logging began to dry up. The depot and siding were removed. (Past image, courtesy of the Nevada Department of Transportation.)

HIGHWAYS

Following World War I, the federal government distributed surplus equipment and supplies to the states for the improvement of highways and roads. The Nevada Department of Highways, the precursor to the Nevada Department of Transportation, received several surplus trucks, including the one pictured here. The writing on the truck reads, "Nevada Highway Dept. No. 633." (Past image, courtesy of the Nevada Department of Transportation.)

The Reno-Carson City Highway was one of the first state highways designated by the Nevada Department of Highways in 1917. At the time, it was part of State Route 3, which ran from Reno to the California state line, near Lida, by way of Carson City, Minden, Yerington, and Goldfield. This portion of the highway, located south of Reno, became part of US 395 and was widened significantly. (Past image, courtesy of Nevada Department of Transportation.)

State Route 3, also called the Reno–Carson City Highway, followed the same general routing as an old wagon road noted as the "Road from Washoe City to Steamboat Springs" on General Land Office maps. Following the formation of the Department of Highways, this particular portion was one of the first sections of highway to be paved in the state with a 6.5-inch-thick concrete. The older alignment was abandoned in the early 1930s for the current one. (Past image, courtesy of Nevada Department of Transportation.)

RENO - CARSON CITY HIGHWAY

Reno-Carson City Highway was part of the Pioneer Branch of the Lincoln Highway. The Pioneer Branch was popular for its aesthetic qualities. Through Washoe Valley, the highway offers views of the Sierra Nevada. Slide Mountain can be seen in the background. This view of the mountain from the highway is still preserved today. (Past image, courtesy of the Nevada Department of Transportation.)

Prior to constructing the highway, the road from Reno to Carson City followed a similar route as the Virginia & Truckee Railroad. Landowners along both the east and west sides of Washoe Lake campaigned for the highway. The state highway chairman, W.B. Alexander, favored the east side of the lake and was ultimately dismissed by Gov. Emmet D. Boyle, who favored the west side. Ultimately, the west side was chosen for the highway. (Past image, courtesy of the Nevada Department of Transportation.)

In the 1930s, the Reno-Carson City Highway became part of US 395, a major highway that runs from Spokane, Washington, to San Diego, California, via Reno and Carson City. The alignment along this portion of the highway remains largely unchanged; however, it has been widened significantly. (Past image, courtesy of the Nevada Department of Transportation.)

The early Reno-Carson City Highway was constructed using convict labor. The early highway required significant maintenance due to heavy winters, the agricultural industry, and the amount of railroad crossings throughout the valley. The c. 1920s realignment required a number of land acquisitions from ranchers, including the Feretto and L.A.L. Green ranches. (Past image, courtesy of the Nevada Department of Transportation.)

This image was taken from what is now the off-ramp of I-580 in north Carson City. The off-ramp was once part of the Reno-Carson City Highway, officially called State Route 3. Historic maps note that a small community called Lakeview and a tollhouse were located here. In 1903, the section house for the Virginia & Truckee Railroad was complete, and a spur of the railroad ran relatively along the same route as the highway. (Past image, courtesy of the Nevada Department of Transportation.)

The land surrounding Lakeview was mostly agricultural, with owners that included the List Cattle Company, the Curtis Wright Corporation, and E.F. and C.M. Hubbard. The highway department reconstructed the highway around the community of Lakeview to include an interchange leading to Washoe Lake. (Past image, courtesy of the Nevada Department of Transportation.)

In 1926, portions of the Lincoln Highway were cosigned US 50. By the mid-1940s, the amount of traffic that moved between Carson City and Lake Tahoe along the Clear Creek Grade had increased from 219 to 961. As a result, the highway department decided to move US 50 just north of the historic grade, as it provided a safer route between Carson City and Lake Tahoe. (Past image, courtesy of the Nevada Department of Transportation.)

Prior to Clear Creek Grade, the Lincoln Highway ran along Kings Canyon Road, located north of the current highway. In 1863, Kings Canyon Road was a toll road. After the turn of the 20th century, Carson City's Good Roads Association took over maintenance of the roadway. The Kings Canyon route was moved to Clear Creek Grade in 1928. (Past image, courtesy of the Nevada Department of Transportation.)

Kings Canyon Road met up with the Clear Creek toll road at Spooner's Summit and continued on to the community of Glenbrook. Maintaining King's Canyon Road proved to be a lot of work for the highway department. Until the decision to move the highway to the old toll road, Clear Creek Grade had largely been used to transport lumber. Following its construction, the new highway had hand-laid rubble walls in sections as well as irrigation ditches and concrete water tanks. These are largely still intact, although most are obscured by overgrown plants. (Past image, courtesy of the Nevada Department of Transportation.)

Construction of the new highway required substantial cut and fill of the old toll road as well as clearing of trees and brush. The highway consisted of a four-inch-thick gravel surface with two nine-foot travel lanes. It opened in 1928. The present-day photograph shows the original alignment and general width of the roadway as intact. (Past image, courtesy of the Nevada Department of Transportation.)

This image, taken from US 50 near Spooner Summit, is facing west towards Carson City. The highway was realigned again to the north, with construction beginning in 1956. Clear Creek Grade is no longer used for highway travel; it is only for private access or US Forest Service. (Past image, courtesy of the Nevada Department of Transportation.)

Clear Creek Grade was continually maintained throughout the 1930s. Improvements were made in 1934 that included amenities for travelers. Many of the cuts and fills are still present, resulting in a preserved historic routing; however, portions of this segment of the highway are susceptible to erosion and rock slides. (Past image, courtesy of the Nevada Department of Transportation.)

Pictured is Clear Creek Grade as it ascends into Carson City, facing east. When Clear Creek Grade became part of the Lincoln Highway, funding for the construction and maintenance of the old highway was provided in large part by the Lincoln Highway Association. The association continued to provide funding, even after the formation of the highway department until 1937, when the association discontinued promotion of the highway. (Past image, courtesy of the Nevada Department Transportation.)

Construction of US 50 during the 1950s included four lanes, measuring approximately 74 feet wide. The design of the highway included no significant sharp turns and enabled easier snow removal, resulting in a more reliable route during the winter months. (Past image, courtesy of the Nevada Department of Transportation.)

This photograph was taken near the intersection of US 395 and US 50 facing west. Survey crews analyze the topography of US 50 to determine the best possible routing of the new highway alignment. This area would become home to Costco, Bodine's Casino, and Fuji Park. (Past image, courtesy of the Nevada Department of Transportation.)

CHAPTER 4

AGRICULTURE

Agriculture was an important industry for the larger Carson City area. Commercial ranching and farming operations developed in the early 1860s. As mining efforts were abandoned, farms began using former mining ditches for irrigation. Farmers planted orchards and grain fields in addition to reining in cattle and sheep. (Past image, courtesy of the Nevada Department of Transportation.)

This c. 1920s photograph shows Prison Road leading up to the Nevada State Prison, which is visible in the background. Prison Road, also called Fifth Street, runs from Carson Street to the prison. Much of the land adjacent to the road was used for cattle ranching, with Fifth Street running through Lompa Ranch. As Carson City expanded, development of I-580 through the eastern part of Carson City removed much of the agricultural setting in this area. (Past image, courtesy of Nevada Department of Transportation.)

North of Carson City along the Reno-Carson Highway, land was used for agricultural purposes in the early days. Successful ranchers established operations in Washoe Valley in the 1850s and 1860s. The name on the mailbox reads "Bersani." Henry Bersani sold part of his land to the state for the construction of State Route 3. (Past image, courtesy of Nevada Department of Transportation.)

Many ranchers planted orchards after establishing their ranches, largely because trees took years to produce fruit; and ranchers could focus on other operations while their crops grew. Fruit was in high demand, and orchards became a standard part of most ranches in the Washoe, Carson, and Eagle Valleys, which continued well into the early 20th century. (Past image, courtesy of the Nevada Department of Transportation.)

Following the decommission of the Virginia & Truckee Railroad and the construction of the I-580 freeway, ranches became a thing of the past, with ranchers dividing up and selling off their land. Most ranch owners around Carson City grew alfalfa, barley, and wheat, in addition to fruit. (Past image, courtesy of the Nevada Department of Transportation.)

Despite significant development throughout Washoe Valley, much of the land retains the historic character from when it was first settled. Construction of I-580 through the valley (located in the center background of present-day photograph) had little impact on the area visually, and the land still retains its historic agricultural setting. (Past image, courtesy of the Nevada Department of Transportation.)

Beef and dairy cattle were another economic mainstay of many ranchers in the area. With the addition of production of hay, grains, dairy, beef, and produce, as well as the development of railroads and highways through the area to transport them, allowed for market expansion of the agricultural industry. Changes in technology and an increase in population shifted how agricultural lands were used, making way for suburban development and commercial complexes. (Past image, courtesy of the Nevada Department of Transportation.)

Jack's Valley, seen from the Clear Creek Grade of the Lincoln Highway, contained the Schneider, Ascuaga, and Johnson ranches. Over the years, ranch land was sold off and portions became tribal land, as well as the Clear Creek Golf Course and homesite. (Past image, courtesy of the Nevada Department of Transportation.)

CHAPTER 5

AROUND TOWN

Carson City's West Side Historic District lies just west of the capitol grounds and Carson Street. The district contains some of Carson City's oldest residences, as well as churches, businesses, and, at one point, schools. (Past image, courtesy of the Nevada Department of Transportation.)

Bowers Mansion is situated at the base of the Carson Range in Washoe Valley, north of Carson City. It was constructed by Sandy and Eilley Bowers between 1862 in the Italianate style. The Bowers were heavily involved in Nevada's mining industry, from which they grew their wealth. The grounds of the estate include a circular driveway with a large, tiered fountain at the center, several outbuildings, and gardens. Washoe County Parks took possession of the grounds in 1965. (Past image, author's collection.)

The Orion House was the home of Orion Clemens, an attorney and the brother of Samuel Clemens, also known as Mark Twain. Twain was a frequent visitor of the home, which is located on Division Street near downtown Carson City. The building was constructed in 1862 in the Victorian style and remains largely unchanged. (Past image, author's collection.)

The Nevada State Prison was established in 1862, just east of Carson City. At the time, much of the adjacent land was agricultural. As Carson City expanded, development of I-580 through the eastern part of Carson City would remove much of the agricultural setting around the prison. (Past image, courtesy of Nevada Department of Transportation.)

The main thoroughfare through town is Carson Street. When the Lincoln Highway was established in 1913, the earliest iteration of the highway was routed through Nevada via Reno down to Carson City. At the time, this branch of the highway was called the Pioneer Branch. The Lincoln Highway Association installed wayfinding signs and painted route markers on trees and poles along the highway. When the association stopped promoting the highway during the 1930s, these signs were removed. (Past image, courtesy of the Nevada Department of Transportation.)

The Warren Engine Company No. 1 building, located at the corner of Musser Street and Curry Street, was constructed in 1863 of locally quarried sandstone. At the time, it served as the Curry Engine House. The bell tower was added around 1907, and shortly after, Warren Engine Company No. 1 took possession of the building. Today, the building adjoins the secretary of state building. The bell tower was removed, and the stone tower was shortened. (Past image, author's collection.)

St. Peter's Episcopal Church was constructed around 1867 in the Gothic Revival style with a cruciform plan. Alterations to the church took place in 1875 and in 1911. Following a small fire, the steeple was reconstructed using fiberglass. The building to the south of the church was constructed in 1867 as a private residence and was purchased in 1961 by the church to serve as the rectory. (Past image, author's collection.)

Early photographs show Carson City to be mostly flat with very little shade or tree coverage. As the town developed and laid out a more permanent town plan, residents planted trees and gardens to provide shade and beautify their properties. This is still evident in the earliest neighborhoods around Carson City and is an important characteristic of them. (Past image, courtesy of the Nevada Department of Transportation.)

Fences and walls defined many of the early residences. White picket fences, tall unpainted fences, and decorative iron fencing were all popular during the late 1800s and early 1900s. During the 1930s, decorative stone fences became popular. Only a few examples of these remain within the neighborhoods today. (Past image, courtesy of the Nevada Department of Transportation.)

Landscaping within the West Side neighborhood has largely remained the same. The preservation of the mature trees has provided a dramatic border between the residential neighborhood and the more commercial parts of Carson City, softening the modern features along many of the streets. (Past image, courtesy of Nevada Department of Transportation.)

When planning the city in 1860, neighborhood streets were laid out 66 feet wide to provide enough space for the turning of wagon trains and to also give the appearance of larger plots and the perceived size of the city. As changes to infrastructure took place, the width of streets was reduced to accommodate sidewalks, curbs, and other features. (Past image, courtesy of the Nevada Department of Transportation.)

Streets around the residential neighborhood were mostly unpaved until the 1950s. In the late 1940s, the highway department began constructing sidewalks, driveway approaches, and engineered drainage in portions of the West Side neighborhood. (Past image, courtesy of the Nevada Department of Transportation.)

The more genteel residences installed sidewalks, mounting blocks (center of historic photograph and to the right of the roadway), or carriage stones prior to the city and state constructing more standardized sidewalks. Early sidewalks were constructed using concrete and varied in width and height. More modern landscaping trends have altered many of the sidewalks in Carson City; however, concrete mounting blocks are still present in the West Side neighborhood. (Past image, courtesy of Nevada Department of Transportation.)

Taken from Third Street near the intersection of Division Street, the Sears-Ferris House can be seen to the right. George Washington Gale Ferris Sr., who owned a nursery in Carson City, is responsible for the abundance of trees in the West Side neighborhood. Ferris was awarded the landscaping contract for the capitol in 1876. (Past image, courtesy of the Nevada Department of Transportation.)

Carson Street was the commercial center of the Carson City area. Early businesses along Carson Street included groceries, hotels, general merchandise stores, liveries, butchers, laundries, candy shops, saloons, tailors, and bakeries, among others. In the later years, Carson Street would be home to auto garages, casinos, more hotels, and restaurants, showing the change in needs from locals and the influence of tourism through the area. (Past image, author's collection.)

This photograph was taken from the intersection of Carson Street and Spear Street looking south. Businesses along Carson Street possessed a variety of architectural styles, including Italianate, Victorian, Spanish Baroque, and Classical Revival. Over time, exterior changes to some of the buildings were in keeping with more modern architectural influences, such as Art Deco or Mid-Century. Although not taken from the exact intersection, the present-day photograph highlights the variation in architectural styles. (Past image, author's collection.)

CARSON ST. LOOKING SOUTH   CARSON CITY NEV.

The Carson City Public School is pictured in 1874 between King Street and Musser Street, near the capitol building. Like many of the city's early structures, the building was constructed using stone from the prison quarry. In 1939, a separate school was built to house high school students on land that is now Bordewich-Bray Elementary. The city ultimately demolished the 1874 school building due to its proximity to an earthquake fault and the belief that it would not be able to withstand such a disaster. (Past image, author's collection.)

Historic RINCKEL MANSION
Carson City, Nevada

The Rinckel Mansion was built by Mathias Rinckel around 1875 in the Italianate style. Rinckel became wealthy during the mining and logging boom. He owned a significant amount of Carson City real estate and added ranching to his long list of lucrative business dealings. Over the years, the home has been a movie set, a museum, and a wedding chapel. It was sold in 2021 with the intention of operating as a bed and breakfast. (Past image, author's collection.)

CHAPTER 6

TOURISM, ENTERTAINMENT, AND RECREATION

A group of men play golf along the shores of Lake Tahoe. Lake Tahoe has always been a recreational favorite for locals and tourists. Many tourists travel through Carson City on their way to the historic lake. (Past image, courtesy of Nevada Department of Transportation.)

The earliest hot springs were established in Carson City by 1861 and included minimal structures outside of a natural spring. By 1907, the hot springs had been developed significantly to include a Mission-style clubhouse, saloon, wood-framed grill, cistern and tank house, private baths, and a pool. Motel units were later added in 1954. Today, the hot springs have been modernized extensively and no longer include many of their historic structures. (Past image, courtesy of Nevada Department of Transportation.)

TOURISM, ENTERTAINMENT, AND RECREATION

This is a view of the intersection of Carson Street and Spear Street looking east. The Nugget Casino was opened in 1954 by Richard Graves. Graves sold the casino shortly after, and the new owners continued to expand the casino by purchasing other buildings along the block. The Nugget was home to the famous Awful Awful burger, consisting of two beef patties and four slices of cheese. (Past image, author's collection.)

Looking north on Carson Street to Proctor Street around the 1970s, the Silver Spur can be seen on the left and the Nugget can be seen in the right background. Many of the buildings along this block were constructed in the late 1880s and have experienced minimal changes to their exterior. Prior to being the Silver Spur Casino, this building housed Tommy's Victory Club, also a casino. Today, the building is operated as a restaurant. (Past image, author's collection.)

TOURISM, ENTERTAINMENT, AND RECREATION

The El Ranch O'tel was originally constructed as a cottage court along US 395/US 50 on the north side of Carson City and consisted of individual cottages. The motel was enlarged in the 1940s to include 14 units as well as a main office and lobby. The motel had a Western theme with knotty pine. It was demolished in the late 1980s and replaced with a strip mall and parking lot. (Past image, author's collection.)

The Silver Queen at 201 Caroline Street is located at the corner of Caroline Street and Curry Street, one block off US 50 in downtown Carson City. The motel was constructed in 1966 and had three stories with Mid-century details, such as the rock veneer and attached neon signage. The motel consisted of 34 rooms with air-conditioning, hot water, televisions, and phones. Today, the building still operates as the Silver Queen Inn. (Past image, author's collection.)

TOURISM, ENTERTAINMENT, AND RECREATION

The Frontier Motel, located along US 50 in northern Carson City, was originally constructed as a motor court with individual cabins and featured stalls and corrals for horses. The motel was updated in the 1950s with a two-story building that included both rooms for rent and commercial retail space. Over time, the building's exterior siding and roofing was updated; however, the motel, which is now vacant, still retains its original sign. (Past image, author's collection.)

GATEWAY MOTEL, NEWEST AND FINEST IN CARSON CITY, NEVADA
THE NATION'S SMALLEST CAPITAL

The Gateway Motel was constructed in 1948 along US 50 in the southern part of Carson City. The motor motel had a U-shaped layout with 27 connected units. Motel registration was located in a separate building at the center of the property. Today, the motel operates as The Lander. (Past image, author's collection.)

TOURISM, ENTERTAINMENT, AND RECREATION

The Victorian, located at the corner of Second Street and Curry Street in downtown Carson City, was restored from an 1870s wedding chapel. The building in the left background was constructed in 1870 and moved to this location around 1900. The building in the right background is thought to have been constructed in 1862 and may have served as a stagecoach stop. Today, the buildings house independent businesses, and the large neon sign has been removed. (Past image, author's collection.)

Located along Clear Creek Road is a painted sign that reads, "Bryan or McKinley for President / F.W. Day Dry Goods." The sign references the presidential campaign of 1896 between William McKinley and William Jennings Bryan. F.W. Day was a mercantile store in Carson City. The sign has been improved many times over the years but has also experienced significant vandalism. (Past image, courtesy of Nevada Department of Transportation.)

Early automobile associations promoted portions of Lincoln Highway between Carson City and Lake Tahoe as some of the most scenic drives in the country. The new scenic Clear Creek Grade opened in the summer of 1928, and it quickly became a popular route, with a 74 percent increase in traffic between 1928 and 1929. It would remain so until the late 1950s. (Past image, courtesy of the Nevada Department of Transportation.)

In 1956, the highway department constructed a new four-lane highway just north of Clear Creek Grade, and the old segment was relinquished to outside parties. The old segment now bisects private land, tribal land, or land managed by the US Forest Service. (Past image, courtesy of the Nevada Department of Transportation.)

TOURISM, ENTERTAINMENT, AND RECREATION

During the 1930s, the highway department installed amenities along Clear Creek Grade to attract visitors to the area, including campgrounds and scenic pullouts. This image was taken from the road leading out of a campground located along Clear Creek, west of Carson City. The campground included camping spaces, latrines, and rubble fireplaces. Following the realignment of the highway through this area, the campground was abandoned. (Past image, courtesy of the Nevada Department of Transportation.)

Farther west of the campground, the highway department constructed a scenic pullout along a hairpin turn as well as a rock drinking fountain and a rubble water tank (left, out of frame). Despite the realignment of the highway, the drinking fountain and water tank are still present along the hairpin turn. These amenities were installed as part of the National Recovery Highway federal relief program. (Both images, courtesy of the Nevada Department of Transportation.)

TOURISM, ENTERTAINMENT, AND RECREATION

Taken from State Route 28 near Incline Village, this historic photograph's caption reads, "Road to Brockway." Many people traveled through Carson City to Lake Tahoe, as Mount Rose Highway had not yet been constructed. At the time, Brockway was a hot springs resort run by Frank Brockway Alverson and his wife. The Alversons had purchased Campbell's Hot Spring from William Campbell in 1900. Over time, the resort also included a casino, a swimming pool, and a dining room. Today, the area mostly contains residential developments. (Past image, courtesy of the Nevada Department of Transportation.)

This photograph was taken from State Route 28 just north of Skunk Harbor. This area was historically part of logging operations. Early topographic maps show a railroad grade leading from the Glenbrook waystation area to Spooner. As industrial operations ceased in Lake Tahoe, the area became a recreational haven for tourists and locals. On any given day during the summer months, cars line the highway and lake goers line the beaches. (Past image, courtesy of the Nevada Department of Transportation.)

TOURISM, ENTERTAINMENT, AND RECREATION

Another recreational spot near Carson City is Washoe Lake. The name Washoe comes from the area's earliest inhabitants, the Washoe people. The discovery of the Comstock Lode in 1859 and the arrival of Mormon settlers in the area dramatically changed the valley. Washoe Lake State Park was established in 1977 as a means to preserve the area. (Past image, courtesy of the Nevada Department of Transportation.)

The Lake Tahoe area is also notable for its winter recreational activities. West of Carson City, the former White Hills Ski Area sits near the intersection of US 50 and State Route 28 above Glenbrook. The ski area was established in 1946, directly adjacent to US 50. Parking was located along US 50, which was widened in 1947 to improve snow removal and allow for additional parking at the hill. (Past image, courtesy of the Nevada Department of Transportation.)

TOURISM, ENTERTAINMENT, AND RECREATION

Development for the ski area began to take shape when the Douglas County Ski Club paid $25 for membership into the California Ski Association, leading to an investment worth $50,000. A T-bar was constructed with steel towers, a lodge, and a ski jump. (Past image, courtesy of the Nevada Department of Transportation.)

Interest in developing the area as a ski hill had increased quickly. The Carson and Douglas Ski Club had advocated and promoted the area as being comparable to that of Mount Rose Ski Bowl, north of Carson City. The group sought aid from not only the Carson City Chamber of Commerce, but residents, local businesses, and the US Forest Service. (Past image, courtesy of the Nevada Department of Transportation.)

TOURISM, ENTERTAINMENT, AND RECREATION

White Hills Ski Area closed in 1952, only a few years after it opened. Following the closure of the ski area, the ski lodge was used a dining hall and recreation room for a prison Conservation Honor Camp program in charge of mistletoe removal in the area. By the 1990s, many of the runs had been overgrown with trees, and the ski lodge was replaced with a forest service fire station. (Past image, courtesy of the Nevada Department of Transportation.)

DISCOVER THOUSANDS OF LOCAL HISTORY BOOKS FEATURING MILLIONS OF VINTAGE IMAGES

Arcadia Publishing, the leading local history publisher in the United States, is committed to making history accessible and meaningful through publishing books that celebrate and preserve the heritage of America's people and places.

Find more books like this at
www.arcadiapublishing.com

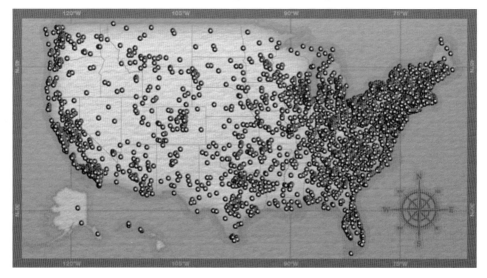

Search for your hometown history, your old stomping grounds, and even your favorite sports team.

Consistent with our mission to preserve history on a local level, this book was printed in South Carolina on American-made paper and manufactured entirely in the United States. Products carrying the accredited Forest Stewardship Council (FSC) label are printed on 100 percent FSC-certified paper.

MADE IN THE USA